鲜香惹味
广东菜

梁绮玲 编著

蒸馔
Steaming

广东省出版集团
广东科技出版社
· 广州 ·

图书在版编目（CIP）数据

蒸馔 / 梁绮玲编著 . —广州：广东科技出版社，2012.8
（鲜香惹味广东菜）
ISBN 978-7-5359-5718-4

Ⅰ.①蒸… Ⅱ.①梁… Ⅲ.①粤菜—蒸菜—菜谱 Ⅳ.① TS972.182.65

中国版本图书馆 CIP 数据核字（2012）第 131261 号

本书中文简体版由香港万里机构出版有限公司授权广东科技出版社在中国内地出版发行。
广东省版权局著作权合同登记
图字：19-2012-044 号

责任编辑：	姚　芸　刘　耕　赵雅雅
美术编辑：	柳国雄
责任校对：	蒋鸣亚
责任印制：	罗华之
出版发行：	广东科技出版社
	（广州市环市东路水荫路 11 号　邮政编码：510075）
E-mail:	gdkjzbb@21cn.com
Http:	//www.gdstp.com.cn
经　　销：	广东新华发行集团股份有限公司
印　　刷：	东莞市翔盈印务有限公司
	（东莞市东城区莞龙路柏洲边路段　邮政编码：523113）
规　　格：	889mm×1 194mm　1/32　印张 3　字数 70 千
版　　次：	2012 年 8 月第 1 版
	2012 年 8 月第 1 次印刷
定　　价：	12.00 元

如发现因印装质量问题影响阅读，请与承印厂联系调换。

忙人、懒人、达人的健康美食攻略

面对大都市快节奏、高压力的生活现状，我们推出了这套《鲜香惹味广东菜》，以**省时、省事、省心、好味、营养**为特色，倡导简约、时尚、健康的饮食理念。书中囊括了广东菜最常见的蒸、炒、煲、炆、煮、炖等烹饪方法，以一日三餐的居家菜为主，强调以味为先，清而不淡，浓而不腻，注重时令，健康为尚。

书中所选食谱均为简单易学，又精致地道的广东特色菜。除了有材料、调料和做法的详细介绍，还包括食材的选购和基本处理方法、常用技巧等技术要点；同时提供每款菜的烹饪时间、人数参考等信息。中英文对照的呈现形式，给即将到国外留学、远离家乡的朋友们提供了不错的参考。"美食达人心动试味"及"Tips"栏目的居家烹饪心得，细致、周到又贴心。

《鲜香惹味广东菜》为都市里的**忙人、懒人、达人**精心设计了一套全面的健康美食攻略，解决您舌尖上的种种疑问，达成您舌尖上的美好愿望。

目录 Contents

看图买材料 Buy ingredients according to the pictures	1
买回来的材料怎样处理？What to do with the ingredients?	5
蒸 Steam	8
一餐中各种食物的摄取比例 The proportion of different food intake during a meal	8
看颜色食果蔬 Choose vegetables and fruit according to colour	9

开始蒸馔 Start steaming

水产 Aquatic

清蒸海上鲜 Steamed fish	11
海鲜扒蛋白 Steamed egg white with seafood	13
榄角蒸鱼腩 Steamed fish belly with preserved olives	15
冬菜蒸龙脷柳 Steamed basa fillet with spiced cabbage	17
面酱蒸狮子鱼 Steamed lion fish with fermented bean paste	19
柠檬蒸乌头 Steamed mullet with lemon	21
鸡油蒸奄仔蟹 Steamed roe crab with chicken oil	23
蒸酿蟹盖 Steamed stuffed crab	25
古法蒸蟹砵 Steamed crab casserole, traditional style	27
虾酱蒸鱿鱼筒 Steamed squid with shrimp paste	29
金银蒜蒸开边虾 Steamed shrimps with minced garlic	31
豉汁蒸带子豆腐 Steamed scallops and beancurd with black bean sauce	33
百花蒸酿豆腐 Steamed stuffed beancurd with shrimp	35
鲜虾油豆腐 Fried beancurd with shrimp	37

家禽 Poultry

家常蒸鸡 Homemade steamed chicken	39
古法蒸鸡翼 Traditional style steamed chicken wing	41
电饭煲盐焗鸡 Rice cooker salt-roasted chicken	43
醉鸡 Drunken chicken	45
龙穿凤翼 Stuffed chicken wings	47

张勤良
2017年购于美国

话梅蒸鸡翼 Steamed chicken wing with plum	49
酸梅蒸鸭片 Steamed duck with plum	51
鲜鸡云腿冬菇块 Steamed chicken and ham with mushroom	53
虾米蒸水蛋 Steamed egg with dried shrimp	55
海鲜茶碗蒸 Steamed cup custard with seafood	57

猪牛 Pork and Beef

梅菜蒸肉片 Steamed pork slice with preserved cabbage	59
土鱿蒸肉饼 Steamed minced pork with dried squid	61
榨菜蒸牛肉 Steamed beef with preserved vegetable	63
豉汁蒸排骨 Steamed spare ribs in black bean sauce	65
肉碎蒸豆腐 Steamed beancurd with minced pork	67
咸鱼蒸肉丸 Steamed salted fish with meat ball	69
酿冬菇 Stuffed dried mushrooms	71

蔬菜 Vegetables

咸猪肉蒸冬瓜夹 Steamed salted pork in winter melon sandwich	73
酿藕片 Steamed stuffed lotus root slices	75
蒜蓉蒸茄子 Steamed eggplant with minced garlic	77
本菇竹荪卷 Steamed bamboo fungus roll with shimeji mushroom	79
三宝酿竹荪 Steamed stuffed bamboo fungus	81
金银蛋蒸豆花 Steamed preserved eggs with beancurd	83

烹饪小词典 Cooking key words

常用调味品（附广东话发音）Common seasonings	86
做菜和味道的常用语 Common phrases of cooking and tastes	90
常用技巧 Common skills	91

看图买材料
Buy ingredients according to the pictures

梅头猪肉（蒸的猪肉）：略带肥肉。
Tenderloin pork (pork for steaming): with some fat.

鲜鸡：肉有光泽。
Chicken: with shiny meat.

牛肉（蒸的牛肉）：瘦肉中有少许肥肉。
Beef (beef for steaming): some fat in the lean meat.

鲩鱼腩：要选色泽鲜明，鳞片无脱落的。
Grass carp belly: colorful, scales are not off.

土鱿：有阵阵鱿鱼香味。
Dried squid: aroma of squid.

乌头：眼睛清晰，鳞片无脱落的。
Mullet: clear eyes, scales are not off.

狮子鱼：选浅黄色的，不要选太鲜黄色。
Lion fish: pick the slightly yellowish instead of the brightly yellowish.

奄仔蟹：眼睛要灵活。
Roe crab (Him Zai): lively eyes.

茄子：表皮光滑，重手。
Eggplant: heavy with smooth skin.

豆腐：要选热或暖的。
Beancurd: pick the hot or warm.

竹荪：无杂质，无霉味。
Bamboo fungus: without impurities and bad smell.

冬菜：浅啡色，有阵阵香味。
Spiced cabbage: light brown and aromatic.

面豉酱：面豉酱可分深色、浅色两种，深色面豉酱一般发酵期较长，味道亦较浓。
Fermented bean paste: there are light and dark pastes. The taste of dark fermented bean paste is richer as the fermentation is longer.

咸柠檬：完整，色泽鲜明。
Salted lemon: intact and bright.

榨菜：内地榨菜较咸，口感较韧。台湾榨菜较淡，口感较硬。
Preserved mustard head: Mainland preserved mustard head is saltier and tough, while Taiwan preserved mustard head more insipid and hard.

榄角：皮薄肉厚，肉纹幼嫩，含油量高，味道芳香。
Preserved olives: thin peel and thick pulp, oily and aromatic.

买回来的材料怎样处理?
What to do with the ingredients?

洗鱼 Wash fish

鱼肚里的黑色膜一定要清洗干净,否则会有腥味。用酒涂抹鱼身,也可除腥味。

The black thin layer in the fish maw must be washed thoroughly, otherwise there'll be fishy small. Smearing wine over the fish can also remove fishy smell.

处理茄子 Handle eggplant

以滚刀法切茄子,茄子切开容易氧化变黑,可放水中略浸。
Cut eggplant into wedges. Eggplant will easily oxidize and turn black, slightly soak in water.

剁猪肉 Chop pork

先切细大剁,即先将猪肉切细再略剁,然后将猪肉搅拌再挞(拍打),边搅拌边加水。

Strip first, that's to cut into strips first and then chop slightly. The other way is to mince the pork first, and then smash. Add water while mincing.

蒸 Steam

原理 Principle
使用高温水蒸气作为传热媒介，利用高热将食材加热至熟。
Heat the ingredients with hot vapor till cooked.

优点 Advantage
保持食材的原汁原味和形态。食材的营养素流失也较少。
Keep the original tastes and shapes of the food. Nutrients loss is less.

一餐中各种食物的摄取比例
The proportion of different food intake during a meal

　　2011年6月美国农业部门（USDA）发表了一套新的"健康饮食指南"以取代有20年历史的膳食金字塔。这套"新饮食指南"以一个圆形餐碟做图示，被称作"我的餐碟"（My Plate）。餐碟被分成4份，分别代表4类食物，每餐食物中有一半是蔬菜及水果，当中蔬菜占较大部分；另外一半则是谷类及蛋白质，而谷类分量比蛋白质稍多。另外还建议一半以上的谷类为全谷物，并且因应年龄需要，每天还要加上1~2份乳制品。

资料来源：chooseMyPlate.gov

看颜色食果蔬
Choose vegetables and fruit according to colour

颜色	植物营养素	例子	功效
红	番茄红素	番茄、红菜头、红辣椒、西瓜、西柚	• 降低患癌风险
红	花青素	红葡萄、红洋葱、草莓、小红莓、山莓	• 抗氧化及消炎,有助消除体内自由基及发炎因子,活化脑细胞 • 保护心脏
橙/黄	α胡萝卜素、β胡萝卜素	番茄、南瓜、胡萝卜、黄辣椒、木瓜、橘子、杏子、柿子	• 保护视力 • 提升免疫力 • 降低患癌及心脏病风险 • 保持黏膜健康
橙/黄	玉米黄素	玉米(粟米)、橘、水蜜桃	• 抗氧化,预防黄斑区受自由基侵害,维护视力健康
橙/黄	维生素C	柠檬、橙、菠萝	• 提升免疫力
橙/黄	叶酸	橙、哈密瓜、芒果	• 负责制造红细胞,预防贫血
绿	叶黄素、玉米黄素	绿豆、芦笋、青椒、菠菜、芥蓝、西兰花、生菜、猕猴桃	• 抗氧化,预防黄斑区受自由基及日光伤害,保护视力 • 降低患癌及心脏病风险
绿	靛基质、异硫氰酸酯	西兰花、椰菜	• 降低患癌风险
绿	有机硫化合物(如蒜辣素)	青葱、韭菜	• 降低患癌风险 • 保护心脏
绿	叶酸	所有绿叶蔬菜,如菠菜、芥蓝等	• 负责制造红细胞,预防贫血
蓝/紫	花青素	茄子、蓝莓、黑莓、紫色葡萄、梅子、无花果	• 抗氧化及消炎,有助消除体内自由基及发炎因子,活化脑细胞 • 保护心脏
白	有机硫化合物(如蒜辣素)	洋葱、蒜头、姜、白萝卜、蘑菇	• 降低患癌风险 • 保护心脏
白	钾质	香蕉、马铃薯	• 稳定血压

开始蒸馔
Start steaming

Aquatic

美食达人心动试味 / Gourmet's Comments

肉质要滑,蒸鱼要计算时间,即蒸即食,不要提早蒸熟。
Time it right to make sure the flesh of the fish is smooth. Serve right after steaming, don't cook too early.

Steamed fish
清蒸海上鲜

⏱ 15 分钟 / Minutes   👥 4 人 / Persons

Tips

1. 蒸鱼要待锅中的水烧至大滚,才把鱼放入;最好预先把碟也蒸热,可以保持鱼的肉质新鲜。
Put the fish into the wok only when the water boils. It would be best to have the dish heated in advance to ensure the freshness of the fish.

2. 蒸鱼要蒸到恰到好处,肉不粘骨为佳,一条约500g重的鱼,约蒸10分钟,以鱼眼凸出、鱼鳍展开为熟。
To make the steamed fish just right, it would be perfect if the fish does not adhere to the bones. For 500 g fish, steam 10 minutes. It's done when the fish eyeballs come out and the fin spreads.

材料　鲈鱼1条（500克）／葱段1汤匙／姜丝1汤匙／葱丝1汤匙／胡椒粉少许
调味　蒸鱼豉油2茶匙

Ingredients　1 bass (500g) / 1 tbsp spring onion / 1 tbsp shredded ginger / 1 tbsp shredded spring onion / dash of pepper
Seasoning　2 tsps steamed fish soy sauce

做法 / Method

1. Cut the bass well, wash and drain it. Slice the fish slightly and dash some pepper on it.

2. Place half of the shredded ginger and spring onion on the dish, and then the bass.

3. Place the steam rack into the wok, add water to nearly the height of the rack. Boil the water, steam the bass over high heat for 10 minutes.

4. Remove from heat, take the bass out. Pour out the water of the steamed fish and remove the ginger and spring onion.

5. Heat 2 tbsps of oil, sauté the shredded ginger, remove from heat. Put in the shredded spring onion and blend with steamed fish soy sauce thoroughly. Ready to serve after pouring it over the bass.

1. 鲈鱼刣好，洗净，沥干水分，鱼身斜剞两刀，抹上少许胡椒粉。

2. 将一半姜丝和葱段铺在蒸碟上，放上鲈鱼。

3. 在锅中放蒸架，加水至接近蒸架高度，烧滚水，将鲈鱼用大火隔水蒸约10分钟。

4. 熄火，取出鲈鱼，倒去碟中鱼汁并除去姜、葱。

5. 另烧热2汤匙油，略爆香姜丝，熄火，下葱丝、蒸鱼豉油拌匀，淋在鲈鱼上即成。

水产 Aquatic

美食达人心动试味 / Gourmet's Comments

蛋质嫩滑,海鲜材料鲜美,要注意颜色搭配。
Smooth egg and fresh seafood. Pay attention to color matching.

Steamed egg white with seafood
海鲜扒蛋白

⏱ 15 分钟 / Minutes 👥 2 人 / Persons

Tips

1. 蒸鸡蛋要用中火,否则鸡蛋会变老。
Steam egg with medium heat, or else the egg will be overdone.

2. 蒸鸡蛋时盖上锡纸,可使鸡蛋蒸熟时更加滑嫩。
Cover the steamed egg with a piece of aluminum foil. This can make the steamed egg even smoother.

材料	鸡蛋白3只 虾仁8只 蟹柳1条 蚬肉20克 清鸡汤½杯 姜2片
调味	生抽少许
腌料	胡椒粉1茶匙 生粉½茶匙 糖½茶匙 盐¼茶匙

Ingredients	3 egg whites / 8 shrimps / 1 crab stick / 20g clams / ½ cup chicken broth / 2 slices ginger
Seasoning	some light soy sauce
Marinades	1 tsp pepper / ½ tsp caltrop starch / ½ tsp sugar / ¼ tsp salt

做法 Method

1. Wash the clams and shrimps respectively, then drain. Marinade for 5 minutes. Wash and drain the crab stick.

2. Stir egg white in a big bowl, mix well with the chicken broth and then pour it into the dish. Cover with a piece of aluminum foil.

3. Place the steam rack into the wok, add water to nearly the height of the rack. Boil the water, steam the egg white over medium heat for 8-10 minutes. Remove from heat and take the egg white out.

4. Heat 2 tbsps of oil, sauté the shredded ginger, stir-fry the shrimps, crab stick and clams until done. And then place them on the cooked egg. Pour some light soy sauce and serve.

1. 蚬肉、虾仁分别洗净，沥干水分，加入腌料腌5分钟。蟹柳洗净，沥干水分。

2. 鸡蛋白放大碗中搅打，加入清鸡汤拌匀，倒入深蒸碟中，盖上锡纸。

3. 在锅中放蒸架，加水至接近蒸架高度，烧滚水，将鸡蛋白用中火隔水蒸8~10分钟至熟。熄火，取出鸡蛋白。

4. 另烧热油2汤匙，爆香姜片，下虾仁、蟹柳和蚬肉炒至熟，放在已蒸熟的鸡蛋白上，淋上少许生抽即成。

Aquatic

美食达人心动试味 / *Gourmet's Comments*

榄角味道芳香，豉油要适量。
Aromatic preserved olives with appropriate amount of soy sauce.

Steamed fish belly with preserved olives
榄角蒸鱼腩

⏱ **18** Minutes 👥 **4** Persons

Tips

1. 要彻底清除鲩鱼腩的黑色薄膜，否则会有腥味。
Thoroughly wash the black thin film of grass carp belly. Otherwise it would taste fishy.

2. 鱼身下放姜、葱，可令鱼与碟之间有空间，令鱼平均受热。
Place spring onion and ginger under the fish so there's some space between the fish and dish, the fish will be heated evenly.

材料	鲩鱼腩1段（400克）／油榄角12粒／葱段1汤匙／姜2片 葱花1汤匙／姜丝½汤匙／陈皮丝1茶匙／油1汤匙 蒸鱼豉油1汤匙／米酒适量
腌料	盐1茶匙／胡椒粉少许

Ingredients	400g grass carp belly／12 preserved olives 1 tbsp sectioned spring onion／2 ginger slices 1 tbsp shredded spring onion／½ tbsp shredded ginger 1 tsp dried citrus peel／1 tbsp oil／1 tbsp steamed fish soy sauce／some rice wine
Marinades	1 tsp salt／some pepper

做法

1. Scale and wash grass carp belly, drain and smear rice wine over the fish, add some marinade.
2. Place the sliced ginger and spring onion on the dish, and then the grass carp belly.
3. Shred the preserved olives. Put the shredded olives, ginger and dried citrus peel on the grass carp belly.
4. Place the steam rack into the wok, add water to nearly the height of the rack. Boil the water, steam the grass carp belly about 12 minutes over high heat.
5. Remove from heat, take out the grass carp belly and add shredded spring onion.
6. Heat 2 tbsps oil, turn off the heat, add steamed fish soy sauce and cook slightly, pour on top of grass carp belly. Serve.

1. 鲩鱼腩去鳞洗净，沥干水分，用米酒抹匀鱼身，下腌料略腌。
2. 将姜片和葱段铺在蒸碟上，放上鲩鱼腩。
3. 油榄角剁碎。将油榄角碎、姜丝、陈皮丝铺在鲩鱼腩上。
4. 在锅中放蒸架，加水至接近蒸架高度，烧滚水，将鲩鱼腩用大火隔水蒸约12分钟。
5. 熄火，取出鲩鱼腩，洒下葱花。
6. 另烧热2汤匙油，熄火，下蒸鱼豉油略煮，淋在鲩鱼腩上即成。

水产 / Aquatic

美食达人心动试味 / Gourmet's Comments

龙鲡柳肉质鲜，粉丝够入味。不要中途开盖，否则会影响温度。

Fresh basa fillet, vermicelli of strong taste. Don't unlid while cooking, otherwise the temperature will be affected.

Steamed basa fillet with spiced cabbage
冬菜蒸龙鲡柳

🕑 15 分钟 / Minutes 👥 4 人 / Persons

Tips

1 龙鲡柳解冻后要立即煮，解冻后不要再放回冰箱，否则肉质会变霉（不新鲜，无弹性）。
Cook right after defrosting, don't put it back into the fridge after defrosting. Otherwise it would be ruined.

2 蒸煮时不要中途打开盖，否则会影响温度。
Don't unlid while cooking, otherwise the temperature will be affected.

材料	龙脷柳2条（400克） 冬菜1汤匙 葱花1汤匙
	蒸鱼豉油1汤匙 粉丝少许 米酒适量 玉米淀粉适量
腌料	盐1茶匙 胡椒粉少许

Ingredients	2 basa fillets (400g) / 1 tbsp spiced cabbage
	1 tbsp shredded spring onion / 1 tbsp steamed fish soy sauce
	some vermicelli / some rice wine / some cornstarch
Marinades	1 tsp salt / some pepper

做法

1. Wash basa fillets after defrosting, drain. Smear rice wine over the fish meat, marinade slightly, coat some cornstarch.

2. Wash the spiced cabbage and drain. Soak vermicelli till soft and drain.

3. Place vermicelli on dish, and then basa fillets, add spiced cabbage over them.

4. Place the steam rack into the wok, add water to nearly the height of the rack. Boil the water, steam the basa fillets over high heat about 8 minutes.

5. Turn off the heat, take out basa fillets and add shredded spring onion.

6. Heat 2 tbsps of oil, turn off the heat, add steamed fish soy sauce and cook slightly, pour on top of basa fillets. Serve.

1. 龙脷柳解冻后洗净，沥干水分，用米酒抹匀鱼肉，下腌料略腌，涂抹少许玉米淀粉。

2. 冬菜洗净，沥干水分备用。粉丝浸软，沥干水分。

3. 将粉丝铺在蒸碟上，放上龙脷柳，冬菜铺在龙脷柳上。

4. 在锅中放蒸架，加水至接近蒸架高度，烧滚水，将龙脷柳用大火隔水蒸约8分钟。

5. 熄火，取出龙脷柳，洒下葱花。

6. 另烧热2汤匙油，熄火，下蒸鱼豉油略煮，淋在龙脷柳上即成。

Aquatic

美食达人心动试味 / Gourmet's Comments

狮子鱼无腥味，有面豉酱味道，但不能过量。
Lion fish has no fishy smell, fermented bean paste is aromatic. But don't add too much.

Steamed lion fish with fermented bean paste
面酱蒸狮子鱼

🕙 10 分钟 / Minutes   👥 4 人 / Persons

Tips

1 用米酒抹鱼身，可去除鱼腥味。
Smear rice wine on the fish to remove the unpleasant smell.

2 加胡椒粉腌鱼，也可除鱼腥味。
Marinade the fish with pepper can also remove unpleasant smell.

材料	狮子鱼800克／葱段1汤匙／姜2片／米酒适量
腌料	面豉酱1汤匙／胡椒粉少许

Ingredients	800g lion fish / 1 tbsp sectioned spring onion / 2 ginger slices / some rice wine
Marinades	1 tbsp fermented bean paste / some pepper

做法

1. Cut and wash lion fish well, drain. Smear rice wine on the fish maw, marinade slightly.
2. Place ginger shreds and sectioned spring onion on dish, and then lion fish.
3. Place steam rack into the wok, add water to nearly the height of the rack. Boil the water, steam the lion fish over high heat about 5 minutes. Turn off the heat, take out lion fish and serve.

1. 狮子鱼刮好洗净，沥干水分，用米酒抹匀鱼肚，下腌料略腌。
2. 将姜切丝，同葱段铺在蒸碟上，放上狮子鱼。
3. 在锅中放蒸架，加水至接近蒸架高度，烧滚水，将狮子鱼用大火隔水蒸约5分钟。熄火，取出狮子鱼即成。

美食达人心动试味 / *Gourmet's Comments*

乌头没有泥味,与柠檬绝配。
There's no mud taste in the mullet, good match with lemon.

Steamed mullet with lemon
柠檬蒸乌头

⏱ 25 分钟 / Minutes 👥 4 人 / Persons

Tips

鱼档上有游水乌头售卖,为咸水乌头,无泥味,肉质鲜美,值得一试。
From time to time fresh mullets are available at fish stalls. They are sea mullets without mud taste. The fish meat is fresh and worth a shot.

| 材料 | 乌头1条（约600克） 姜2片 葱段1汤匙 咸柠檬1个
冬菇丝1汤匙 姜丝½汤匙 红辣椒丝1茶匙 |
| --- | --- |
| 腌料 | 盐1汤匙 |
| 调味 | 糖1汤匙 鱼露1茶匙 绍酒1茶匙 生粉1茶匙 麻油少许
胡椒粉少许 |

| Ingredients | 1 mullet (about 600g) / 2 ginger slices / 1 tbsp sectioned spring onion
1 salted lemon / 1 tbsp shredded dried black mushrooms
½ tbsp shredded ginger / 1 tsp shredded red chili |
| --- | --- |
| Marinade | 1 tbsp salt |
| Seasonings | 1 tbsp sugar / 1 tsp fish sauce / 1 tsp Shaoxin wine
1 tsp cornstarch / some sesame oil / some pepper |

做法 / Method

1. Wash and cut the mullet well. Drain and marinade slightly.
2. Remove the pulp and core of the salted lemon. Shred.
3. Put shredded ginger and spring onion on dish, and then the mullet.
4. Mix the shredded salted lemon, ginger, red chili, mushroom and marinades well, and then place on the mullet.
5. Place steam rack into the wok, add water to nearly the height of the rack. Boil the water, steam the mullet over high heat about 12 minutes. Turn off the heat and take out. Serve.

1. 乌头刏好洗净，沥干水分，下腌料略腌。
2. 咸柠檬去果囊和核，切丝。
3. 将姜片和葱段铺在蒸碟上，放上乌头。
4. 咸柠檬丝、姜丝、红辣椒丝、冬菇丝与调味料拌匀，铺在乌头上。
5. 在锅中放蒸架，加水至接近蒸架高度，烧滚水，将乌头用大火隔水蒸约12分钟，熄火，取出即成。

水产 Aquatic

美食达人心动试味 / *Gourmet's Comments*

蟹肉鲜嫩,一定要购买生猛的蟹,因蟹容易变坏。
To enjoy fresh crab, make sure it's alive when buying as it perishes easily.

Steamed roe crab with chicken oil
鸡油蒸奄仔蟹

25 Minutes | 4 Persons

Tips

鸡油可从鸡皮下取出鸡膏,慢火煎出即可。
Take out the fat under chicken skin, shallow-fry it into oil.

材料	奄仔蟹4只／葱段2棵（的量）／姜片6片／蒜片2粒 鸡油20克／盐适量
蘸汁	浙醋¼杯

Ingredients	4 roe crabs (Him Zai) / 2 sectioned spring onions 6 ginger slices / 2 garlic slices / 20g chicken oil / some salt
For dipping	¼ cup vinegar

做法  Method

1. Wash and cut the crabs well. Drain and cut into pieces. Crack the crab claws slightly.

2. Heat the chicken oil and sauté garlic slices.

3. Put the crab pieces on dish, add ginger slices and shredded spring onion, put some salt on it. Pour chicken oil and garlic slices over.

4. Place steam rack into the wok, add water to nearly the height of the rack. Boil the water, steam the crabs over high heat about 15 minutes. Turn off the heat and take out. Serve with vinegar.

1. 蟹㓥好洗净，沥干水分，斩块，蟹钳略拍碎。

2. 烧热鸡油，爆香蒜片备用。

3. 蟹件放在蒸碟上，加上姜片和葱段，下少许盐，再淋上鸡油和蒜片。

4. 在锅中放蒸架，加水至接近蒸架高度，烧滚水，将蟹用大火隔水蒸约15分钟，熄火，取出，与浙醋同上即成。

Aquatic

美食达人心动试味 / *Gourmet's Comments*

肉碎有蟹味,够鲜甜。
Minced meat with crab aroma. Fresh and sweet.

Steamed stuffed crab
蒸酿蟹盖

⏱ **20** Minutes 👥 **4** Persons

Tips

1 蟹购买回家后,若不是马上煮食,要放入冰箱,否则容易变臭。
Put the crab into the fridge if it's not cooked immediately, otherwise it will smell bad easily.

2 余下蟹身可作其他用途,例如煲蟹粥。
The rest of the crab body can be used for other purposes, like cooking crab congee.

| 材料 | 奄仔蟹4只 / 绞猪肉300克 / 鸡蛋1只 |
| 腌料 | 生抽2茶匙 / 生粉1茶匙 / 胡椒粉少许 |

| Ingredients | 4 roe crabs (Him Zai) / 300g minced pork / 1 egg |
| Marinades | 2 tsps soy sauce / 1 tsp cornstarch / some pepper |

做法 / Method

1. Remove the shells of roe crabs, cut well, brush, wash and drain.

2. Slightly marinade the minced pork for 15 minutes, add egg and mix, then stuff it into the crab shells. Place crab shells on dish.

3. Place steam rack into the wok, add water to nearly the height of the rack. Boil the water, steam the stuffed crab over high heat about 10 minutes. Turn off the heat and take out. Serve.

1. 奄仔蟹拆下蟹盖,刣好,刷洗净,沥干水分备用。

2. 绞猪肉加腌料略腌15分钟,加入鸡蛋拌匀,酿入蟹盖中。将蟹盖放在蒸碟上。

3. 在锅中放蒸架,加水至接近蒸架高度,烧滚水,将蟹盖用大火隔水蒸约10分钟,熄火,取出即成。

美食达人心动试味 / Gourmet's Comments

蟹汁的鲜味，鸡蛋的嫩滑，加上蒜香和肉粒的提味，能多下三碗饭。

Fresh crab sauce and smooth egg. Arometic garlic and minced meat increase the flavor of dish. It is best served with cooked rice.

Steamed crab casserole traditional style
古法蒸蟹砵

25~30 分钟 Minutes | 4~6 人 Persons

Tips

用保鲜膜包住砵头去蒸，蒸出来的蛋更嫩滑。

While steaming, wrap the container with plastic wrap, can keep the egg more tender and smooth.

材料 花蟹或泥蟹2只，600~720克 免治猪肉250克
鸡蛋2只 蒜蓉2汤匙 青葱粒1汤匙

调味 盐½茶匙 糖1茶匙 胡椒粉适量 生粉/玉米淀粉2茶匙
生油2茶匙 酒2茶匙

Ingredients 2 spotted crabs or mud crabs, 600-720g / 250g ground pork / 2 eggs / 2 tbsps minced garlic / 1 tbsp spring onion, chopped

Seasonings ½ tsp salt / 1 tsp white sugar / some pepper, pinch / 2 tsps cornstarch / 2 tsps peanut oil / 2 tsps cooking wine

做法 Method

1. Wash the crabs. Chop. Crack the pincers.

2. Combine the crab's fat and ground pork. Stir well. Add the seasonings and minced garlic. Stir well. Add the beaten eggs. Whisk until it forms sticky paste. Add the crabs. Stir well.

3. Boil water. Steam the crabs in a casserole over high heat for 15-20 minutes. Then heat the casserole directly over low heat until fragrant, about 5-10 minutes. Sprinkle with some chopped spring onion.

1. 蟹剖洗干净，斩块，蟹钳略拍碎。

2. 把猪肉和蟹膏拌匀，加入调味料和蒜蓉捞匀，再打入鸡蛋拌匀，并搅至起胶，将蟹块放入肉碎内。

3. 烧一锅滚水，放入蟹砵以大火蒸15~20分钟，再把蟹砵直接放在火炉上以慢火烧至飘出香味，5~10分钟，洒上葱粒装饰。

Aquatic

美食达人心动试味 / Gourmet's Comments

阵阵虾酱香味,不能太咸。
Aromatic shrimp paste, don't make it too salty.

Steamed squid with shrimp paste
虾酱蒸鱿鱼筒

⏱ 10 分钟 / Minutes   👥 4 人 / Persons

Tips

1 虾酱若不加糖,味道会太咸。
Shrimp paste will be too salty without adding sugar.

2 鱿鱼筒不要蒸得过火,否则会变韧。
Squid will be hard if overdone.

| 材料 | 鱿鱼筒350克 / 葱花½汤匙 |
| 腌料 | 虾酱1汤匙 / 糖1茶匙 / 胡椒粉少许 |

| Ingredients | 350g squid / ½ tbsp chopped spring onion |
| Marinades | 1 tbsp shrimp paste / 1 tsp sugar / some pepper |

做法 Method

1. Wash and drain the squid.
2. Add sugar in shrimp paste and mix well. Slightly marinade squid with shrimp paste and pepper for 15 minutes.
3. Place steam rack into the wok, add water to nearly the height of the rack. Boil the water, steam the squid over high heat about 4 minutes. Turn off the heat and take out. Add spring onion and serve.

1. 鱿鱼筒洗净，沥干水分。
2. 虾酱下糖拌匀。鱿鱼筒加虾酱、胡椒粉略腌15分钟。
3. 在锅中放蒸架，加水至接近蒸架高度，烧滚水，将鱿鱼筒用大火隔水蒸约4分钟，熄火，取出，加葱花即成。

水产 / Aquatic

美食达人心动试味 / Gourmet's Comments

炸蒜蓉味道够香，但不能炸炆。
Fried minced garlic is aromatic, but do not overdo it.

Steamed shrimps with minced garlic
金银蒜蒸开边虾

⏱ 10 分钟 / Minutes　　👥 4 人 / Persons

Tips

1. 中虾可改为青口、带子、蛏子等贝壳类。
Medium shrimps can be substituted by other shellfish such as mussels, scallops and razor clams.

2. 从虾的背部划一刀，很容易开边。
Slightly cut at the back of shrimps, it's easy to cut into halves.

材料	中虾480克 / 蒜蓉3汤匙 / 葱花1汤匙
腌料	盐1茶匙 / 胡椒粉少许
调味	蒸鱼豉油2汤匙 / 油1汤匙

Ingredients	480g medium shrimps / 3 tbsps mince garlic / 1 tbsp chppoed spring onion
Marinades	1 tsp salt / some pepper
Seasonings	2 tbsps steam fish soy sauce / 1 tbsp oil

做法 Method

1. Shell the shrimps and keep the tails. Devein and cut into halves. Wash and drain. Add marinades and mix well. Place the shrimps on dish.

2. Place steam rack into the wok, add water to nearly the height of the rack. Boil the water, steam the medium shrimps over high heat about 5 minutes. Turn off the heat and take out. Discard the water.

3. Heat the oil, add half of the minced garlic and deep-fry till aromatic, put it over the medium shrimps and add chopped spring onion.

4. Heat the oil again, add the rest of minced garlic and shallow-fry, turn off the heat. Add steam fish soy sauce and slightly cook, pour on the shrimps and serve.

1. 虾去壳留尾部，去肠，开边，洗净，沥干水分，下腌料拌匀略腌，将虾铺在蒸碟上。

2. 在锅中放蒸架，加水至接近蒸架高度，烧滚水，将中虾用大火隔水蒸约5分钟。熄火，取出，倒去水分。

3. 另烧热油，下一半蒜蓉炸香，放在中虾上，洒下葱花。

4. 再烧滚油，下另一半蒜蓉略炒，熄火，下蒸鱼豉油略煮，淋在中虾上即成。

Aquatic

美食达人心动试味 / Gourmet's Comments

要豆腐嫩滑,一定要用软豆腐。
To have smooth beancurd, use soft beancurd.

Steamed scallops and beancurd with black bean sauce
豉汁蒸带子豆腐

🕙 10 分钟 / Minutes   👥 4 人 / Persons

Tips

1. 豆腐分软和硬两种,软豆腐宜蒸,硬豆腐宜煎。
There are soft and hard pressed beancurds. The soft is for steam, while the hard is for shallow-fry.

2. 可用其他海鲜代替带子。
Scallops can be substituted by other seafood.

材料　带子8只／软豆腐1块／豆豉1茶匙／蒜蓉1茶匙
　　　葱花1茶匙
腌料　胡椒粉少许
调味　蒸鱼豉油1汤匙

Ingredients　8 scallops / 1 piece soft beancurd / 1 tsp black bean
　　　　　　1 tsp minced garlic / 1 tsp chopped spring onion
Marinade　　some pepper
Seasoning　　1 tbsp steam fish soy sauce

做法  Method

1. Wash scallops and drain. Marinade slightly.

2. Wash black bean and drain.

3. Wash beancurd and drain. Cut into 8 pieces.

4. Put beancurd on dish, place a scallop on each beancurd, and then minced garlic and black bean.

5. Place steam rack into the wok, add water to nearly the height of the rack. Boil the water, steam the scallops and beancurd over high heat about 5 minutes. Turn off the heat and take out. Discard water and add chopped spring onion.

6. Heat oil, turn off the heat. Add steam fish soy sauce and slightly cook, pour on the scallops and serve.

1. 带子洗净，沥干水分，下腌料略腌。

2. 豆豉洗净，沥干水分。

3. 豆腐洗净，沥干水分，切成8块。

4. 豆腐放在蒸碟上，每块豆腐上放一粒带子，再铺上蒜蓉和豆豉。

5. 在锅中放蒸架，加水至接近蒸架高度，烧滚水，将带子豆腐用大火隔水蒸约5分钟。熄火，取出，倒去水分，洒上葱花。

6. 另烧热油，熄火，下蒸鱼豉油略煮，淋在带子上面即成。

Aquatic

美食达人心动试味 / Gourmet's Comments

虾胶要够爽口，必须搅至起胶。
Delicious shrimp paste, it must be mixed till elastic.

Steamed stuffed beancurd with shrimp
百花蒸酿豆腐

🕒 15 分钟 / Minutes   👥 4~6 人 / Persons

Tips

1 虾蒸煮前用盐水略浸，可使肉质爽口。
Slightly soak shrimps in salt water before steaming to ensure the texture is elastic.

2 搅拌虾胶时要沿同一个方向，否则不易起胶。
Stir the shrimps in one direction, otherwise it's hard to get elastic.

材料	虾100克 / 软豆腐1块 / 葱花1茶匙 / 玉米淀粉1茶匙 / 盐水适量
腌料	盐1茶匙 / 胡椒粉少许
调味	蒸鱼豉油1汤匙

Ingredients	100g shrimps / 1 piece soft beancurd / 1 tsp chopped spring onion 1 tsp corn starch / some salt water
Marinades	1 tsp salt / some pepper
Seasoning	1 tbsp steam fish soy sauce

做法 / Method

1. Shell and devein the shrimps. Wash and drain. Soak slightly with salt water, and then drain again.

2. Put shrimps on chopping board and slightly pat with the back of knife, chop then. Put it into a big bowl, mix with marinades. Stir in one direction till elastic.

3. Wash the beancurd and drain, cut into 8 pieces and put them on dish. Coat the beancurd surfaces with cornstarch, stuff with shrimp paste.

4. Place steam rack into the wok, add water to nearly the height of the rack. Boil the water, steam the stuffed beancurd over high heat about 8 minutes. Turn off the heat and take out. Pour out the water in dish and add spring onion.

5. Heat the oil, turn off heat. Add steam fish soy sauce and cook slightly, pour over the shrimp paste and serve.

1. 虾去壳去肠，洗净，沥干水分。用盐水略浸，再沥干水分。

2. 虾放在砧板上用刀背略拍，再剁。放在大碗中，下腌料拌匀，顺一个方向用力搅拌至起胶。

3. 豆腐洗净，沥干水分，切成8块，放在蒸碟上，豆腐面上扫上玉米淀粉，酿入虾胶。

4. 在锅中放蒸架，加水至接近蒸架高度，烧滚水，将酿豆腐用大火隔水蒸约8分钟，熄火，取出，倒去碟中水分，加葱花。

5. 烧滚油，熄火，下蒸鱼豉油略煮，淋在虾胶上即成。

Aquatic

美食达人心动试味 / Gourmet's Comments

芦笋鲜嫩，火腿、芦笋长度要一致，材料颜色搭配要鲜艳。
Fresh asparagus. Ham should be as long as asparagus. Ingredients should match with each other in color.

Fried beancurd with shrimp
鲜虾油豆腐

🕐 15 分钟 / Minutes 👥 4 人 / Persons

Tips

1 油豆腐可在超级市场购买。
Fried beancurd is available at supermarket.

2 可因个人口味而用其他配料代替火腿、芦笋。
Ham and asparagus can be substituted by other ingredients according to personal tastes.

材料	鲜虾6只 / 火腿扒1片 / 芦笋6条 / 油豆腐6块 / 韭菜6条
芡汁料	清汤¼杯 / 玉米淀粉1汤匙 / 糖¼茶匙 / 盐¼茶匙

Ingredients	6 shrimps / 1 ham steak / 6 asparagus / 6 dried beancurds / 6 leeks
Thickenings	¼ cup chicken broth / 1 tbsp cornstarch / ¼ tsp sugar / ¼ tsp salt

做法 Method

1. Shell and devein the shrimps. Wash and drain. Wash and drain the ham, strip. Wash asparagus, cut according to the length of the ham.

2. Wash leeks and drain. Boil water in the wok, cook the leeks till soft. Take out and dry.

3. Wash the dried beancurd and drain. Boil water in the wok, blanch the dried beancurd, take out and rinse in cold water, squeeze out the water.

4. Put 1 asparagus, 1 ham and 1 shrimp on fried beancurd, tie up with leeks and put on dish.

5. Boil the water, steam fried beancurd rolls over high heat for about 5 minutes till cooked. Remove from heat and take out, pour out the water.

6. Mix the thickening in the bowl. Heat the wok and pour in the thickening, mix well and cook till transparent, pour it over the dried beancurd rolls and serve.

1. 鲜虾去壳去肠，洗净，沥干水分。火腿扒洗净，沥干水分，切粗条。芦笋洗净，切成火腿条般长度。

2. 韭菜洗净，沥干水分。锅中烧滚水，加入韭菜灼软，取出，压出水分。

3. 油豆腐洗净，沥干水分。锅中烧滚水，加入油豆腐汆水，取出过冷水，压出水分。

4. 把1条芦笋、1条火腿和1只虾放在油豆腐上，用韭菜绑好，放蒸碟上。

5. 烧滚水，将油豆腐卷用大火隔水蒸约5分钟至熟，熄火，取出，倒去水分。

6. 将芡汁料放碗中拌匀。烧热锅，下芡汁料，拌匀，煮成玻璃芡，淋在油豆腐卷上即成。

Poultry

美食达人心动试味 / *Gourmet's Comments*

鸡稍摊凉较容易斩块，也较美观。
It'd be easier to cut if the chicken is cooled down a little bit, it would look better too.

Homemade steamed chicken
家常蒸鸡

🕒 30 分钟 / Minutes   👥 6 人 / Persons

Tips

用长竹签插入鸡髀（鸡腿）最厚部位，能顺利插入表示鸡已熟。
Insert a bamboo stick into the thickest part of the chicken leg, it's done if it can get through.

| 材料 | 光鸡1只 / 干葱头3粒 / 葱丝1杯 / 姜丝¼杯 红辣椒丝½汤匙 / 盐适量 |
| 调味料 | 麻油1汤匙 / 生抽2茶匙 / 沙姜粉½茶匙 |

| Ingredients | 1 chicken / 3 shallots / 1 cup of shredded spring onion / ¼ cup of shredded ginger / ½ tbsp shredded red chili / some salt |
| Marinades | 1 tbsp sesame oil / 2 tsps light soy sauce / ½ tsp mush ginger power |

做法  Method

1. Wash the chicken and drain. Smear salt on the chicken and marinade slightly.

2. Place the steam rack into the wok, add water to nearly the height of the rack. Boil the water, steam the chicken over high heat for 20 minutes. Cool down for a while. Chop and put on dish.

3. Put shredded ginger, spring onion and red chili in bowl and mix.

4. Heat oil in wok, sauté shallots till aromatic and discard. Add the hot oil into the ginger and spring onion, add marinades and mix well. Rinse over the chicken and serve.

1. 光鸡洗净,沥干水分,用盐抹匀鸡身略腌。

2. 在锅中放蒸架,加水至接近蒸架高度,烧滚水,将鸡用大火隔水蒸约20分钟至熟,稍摊凉后斩块上碟。

3. 姜丝、葱丝和红辣椒丝放碗中拌匀。

4. 烧热油锅,下干葱头爆香,弃去干葱头,将滚油溅入混合姜葱料中,加调味料拌匀,淋在鸡上即成。

家禽 Poultry

美食达人心动试味 / Gourmet's Comments

鸡翼没有冷冻味道,枸杞子可增添色彩,但不能下太多,否则有酸味。
There's no frozen taste in the chicken. Wolfberry makes it more colorful. But don't add too many, otherwise it'll be sour.

Traditional style steamed chicken wing
古法蒸鸡翼

⏱ 20 分钟 Minutes　👥 4~6 人 Persons

Tips

1. 鸡翼加姜汁酒腌,可去除冷冻味。
Marinade chicken wings with ginger juice to remove the frozen taste.

2. 云耳要切去硬蒂部分,并洗净去沙。
Cut the stalks of black fungus, wash and remove sand.

材料	鸡翼300克／云耳10克／金针菜（黄花菜）10克／冬菇4只／枸杞子1汤匙／米酒2茶匙
腌料	生抽1汤匙／姜汁2茶匙／酒2茶匙／鱼露1茶匙／糖½茶匙／麻油少许
调味	上汤¼杯／蚝油1汤匙
芡汁	生粉½茶匙／水2汤匙

Ingredients	300g chicken wings / 10g black fungus / 10g dried lily flowers / 4 dried black mushrooms / 1 tbsp wolfberry / 2 tsps rice wine
Marinades	1 tbsp soy sauce / 2 tsps ginger juice / 2 tsps wine / 1 tsp fish sauce ½ tsp sugar / some sesame oil
Seasonings	¼ cup chicken broth / 1 tbsp oyster sauce
Thickenings	½ tsp caltrop starch / 2 tbsps water

做法 / Method

1. Wash the chicken wings (defrost if they are frozen) and drain. Marinade for 10 minutes.
2. Soak thoroughly black fungus, dried lily flowers and dried black mushrooms respectively. Wash and drain. Discard stalks. Cut black fungus into small pieces.
3. Put chicken wings on dish, add marinades in black fungus, dried lily flowers, dried black mushrooms and wolfberries. Mix well and put on chicken wings.
4. Place the steam rack into the wok, add water to nearly the height of the rack. Boil the water, steam the chicken wings over high heat for 8 minutes. Serve.

1. 鸡翼洗净，沥干水分（如用冷冻鸡翼需要预先解冻），下腌料腌10分钟。
2. 云耳、金针菜、冬菇分别浸透，洗净，沥干水分，去蒂。云耳切小朵。
3. 鸡翼放蒸碟上，云耳、金针菜、冬菇、枸杞子加调味料拌匀，放在鸡翼上。
4. 在锅中放蒸架，加水至接近蒸架高度，烧滚水，将鸡翼用大火隔水蒸约8分钟至熟即成。

家禽 Poultry

美食达人心动试味 / Gourmet's Comments

鸡够入味,没有冷冻味道。可同时放入鸡蛋一道焗。
Tasty chicken without frozen taste. Eggs can be roasted together.

Rice cooker salt-roasted chicken
电饭煲盐焗鸡

⏱ 30 分钟 / Minutes   👥 6 人 / Persons

Tips

1. 鸡可用食用砂纸包裹,避免盐附于鸡身。
   Chicken can be wrapped in sandpaper so that there'll be no salt on the chicken.

2. 可同时放入鸡蛋,一道焗成盐焗鸡蛋。
   Eggs can be roasted together to make salt-roasted eggs.

材料 光鸡1只 / 粗盐5汤匙 / 幼盐1汤匙 / 姜3片 / 葱1条
胡椒粉少许

Ingredients 1 chicken / 5 tbsps coarse salt / 1 tbsp fine salt / 3 ginger slices
1 spring onion / some pepper

做法 Method

1. Wash the chicken and drain. Smear fine salt and pepper inside and outside.
2. Wash and stuff ginger and spring onion inside.
3. Wrap the inside of the cooker with aluminum foil, dash coarse salt evenly at the bottom, place the chicken on coarse salt, press the button. Roast till off.
4. Turn the chicken to the other side, press the button again, roast till off, cook for another 5 minutes. When the water dips, the light of rice cooker will be on automatically, roast till off. Take out, cool down slightly. Chop and serve.

1. 光鸡洗净,沥干水分,用幼盐和胡椒粉擦遍全身内外。
2. 姜、葱洗净,塞入鸡腔内。
3. 用锡纸覆盖住电饭煲内锅,将粗盐均匀地铺在锅底,将鸡平放在粗盐上,启动焗至熄火。
4. 将鸡身转向另一面,再启动焗至熄火,再煮5分钟。当水滴落时,电饭煲会自动亮灯,焗至熄火,取出,稍摊凉后斩块上碟。

Poultry 家禽

美食达人心动试味 / *Gourmet's Comments*

把鸡腿卷起时要扎紧,并保持圆条状。
Tie the chicken leg tight when rolling to make it a cylinder.

Drunken chicken
醉鸡

⏱ 90 分钟 / Minutes   👥 6 人 / Persons

Tips

可以鸡扒代替鸡腿,省掉去骨的步骤。
Chicken leg can be substituted by chicken fillet to save the process of removing bones.

材料	鸡腿1只
汤料	枸杞子10粒 / 山药5片 / 桂圆肉5粒 / 人参须少许 / 清水3杯
调味	盐10克 / 米酒20毫升 / 绍兴酒20毫升 / 玫瑰露酒20毫升 / 鸡粉2茶匙

Ingredient	1 chicken leg (boneless)
Soup ingredients	10 wolfberries / 5 Chinese yam slices / 5 dried longans / some ginseng / 3 cups water
Seasonings	10g salt / 20 ml rice wine / 20 ml Shaoxing wine / 20 ml rose wine / 2 tsps chicken powder

做法

1. Wash the chicken leg and remove bones. Wrap into cylinder shape with aluminum foil and tie at both ends. Steam in a pot for 20 minutes. Take out and cool, remove the aluminum foil.

2. Boil the soup ingredients in a pot, and boil over slow heat for another 25 minutes, remove from heat.

3. Wait until the soup is cool, add seasonings and mix. Soak the steamed chicken leg for about 1 day, take out and slice.

1. 鸡腿洗净去骨,用锡纸包卷成圆条形,在两头扎紧,放入锅中隔水蒸20分钟,取出,放凉,撕去锡纸。

2. 汤料放入锅中煮滚,转小火再煮25分钟,熄火。

3. 待汤料冷却,再放入调味料拌匀,将蒸好的鸡腿浸约1天,即可取出切片。

家禽 Poultry

美食达人心动试味 / Gourmet's Comments

无骨,每口都有菜和肉,西芹要去掉根。
Boneless, vegetables and meat in every bite, remove the root of the celery.

Stuffed chicken wings
龙穿凤翼

⏱ 40 分钟 / Minutes 👥 4 人 / Persons

Tips

在鸡翼头尾划开鸡翼的筋,沿鸡骨向下划,再将鸡肉连皮向下推,便很容易将鸡翼去骨。
Cut the vein at both ends of the chicken wing, cut along the chicken bone, push the chicken meat with skin downwards, it's easy to remove bones from the chicken wing.

| 材料 | 鸡中翼10只 / 火腿扒½块 / 西芹1条 / 甘笋（小胡萝卜）1小条 |
| 腌料 | 生抽2茶匙 / 酒1茶匙 / 盐1茶匙 / 老抽1茶匙 / 姜汁1茶匙 / 糖½茶匙 / 胡椒粉少许 |

| Ingredients | 10 chicken wings (middle part) / ½ ham steak / 1 celery / 1 small carrot |
| Marinades | 2 tsps light soy sauce / 1 tsp wine / 1 tsp salt / 1 tsp dark soy sauce / 1 tsp ginger juice / ½ tsp sugar / some pepper |

做法  Method

1. Wash celery, carrot, ham steak respectively, drain and strip.
2. Wash chicken wings and drain (defrost first if frozen), cut the vein at both ends, remove bones.
3. Marinade chicken wings for 15 minutes.
4. Stuff celery, carrot and ham sticks into chicken wings, put on dish in order.
5. Place the steam rack into the wok, add water to nearly the height of the rack. Boil the water, steam the chicken wings over high heat about 13 minutes till cooked. Serve.

1. 西芹、甘笋、火腿扒分别洗净，沥干水分，切成条状。
2. 鸡翼洗净，沥干水分（如用冷冻鸡翼需要预先解冻），切去头尾部分的筋，去骨。
3. 鸡翼加腌料腌15分钟。
4. 将西芹、甘笋、火腿条分别酿入鸡翼内，排在蒸碟上。
5. 在锅中放蒸架，加水至接近蒸架高度，烧滚水，将鸡翼用大火隔水蒸约13分钟至熟即成。

Poultry

美食达人心动试味 / Gourmet's Comments

话梅的甜酸味能增加食欲，但不能下太多。
Sweet and sour preserved plum is appetizing. But don't add too much.

Steamed chicken wing with plum
话梅蒸鸡翼

15 分钟 / Minutes   4 人 / Persons

Tips

1. 金针菜（黄花菜）浸软后要切除硬蒂部位。
   Cut stalks of dried lily flowers after soaking soft.
2. 云耳、金针菜（黄花菜）飞水，可去除霉味。
   Blanch black fungus and dried lily flowers to remove undesired smell.

材料	鸡中翼500克 / 甜话梅5粒 / 金针菜（黄花菜）40克 / 云耳40克 姜2片 葱段1棵量
腌料	姜汁1茶匙 / 酒1茶匙 / 玉米淀粉½茶匙 / 胡椒粉少许
调味	清鸡汤½杯 / 蚝油1汤匙 / 麻油少许

Ingredients	500g chicken wings / 5 sweet preserved plums / 40g dried lily flowers / 40g black fungus / 2 ginger slices / 1 spring onion (sectioned)
Marinades	1 tsp ginger juice / 1 tsp wine / ½ tsp cornstarch / some pepper
Seasonings	½ cup chicken broth / 1 tbsp oyster oil / some sesame oil

做法  Method

1. Soak thoroughly black fungus, dried lily flower. Wash and drain, discard stalks. Cut black fungus into small pieces. Boil water in a wok, blanch black fungus, dried lily flowers respectively, then take out and rinse in cold water, squeeze out the water.

2. Wash and drain chicken wings (defrost first if frozen), Marinade slightly.

3. Cut preserved plums into pieces, discard cores.

4. Place chicken wings on dish, put plums, dried lily flowers, black fugnus on top. Add seasonings and mix.

5. Place the steam rack into the wok, add water to nearly the height of the rack. Boil the water, steam the chicken wings over high heat about 8 minutes till cooked. Serve.

1. 云耳、金针菜分别浸透，洗净，沥干水分，去蒂。云耳切小朵。锅中烧滚水，分别加入云耳、金针菜飞水，取出过冷河，压出水分。

2. 鸡翼洗净，沥干水分（如用冷冻鸡翼需要预先解冻），加入腌料略腌。

3. 话梅起肉切碎。

4. 鸡翼排在蒸碟上，铺上话梅肉、金针菜、云耳，下调味料拌匀。

5. 在锅中放蒸架，加水至接近蒸架高度，烧滚水，将鸡翼用大火隔水蒸约8分钟至熟即成。

Poultry

美食达人心动试味 / *Gourmet's Comments*

鸭要无膻味，汁料应味道适中，梅子要下适量的糖。
To remove the smell of mutton from duck, the thickening should be done right, add some sugar in sour plums.

Steamed duck with plum
酸梅蒸鸭片

⏱ 90 Minutes / 分钟　　👥 6 Persons / 人

Tips

1 鸭的尾部有膻味，可以把尾部两粒鸭子除去。
To remove the smell of mutton of duck tail, remove the textiles of the duck.

2 可用鸡代替鸭。
Duck can be substituted by chicken.

材料	米鸭（一种比较嫩的鸭）1只 / 梅子3粒 / 姜4片 / 葱段2棵量 葱花1汤匙 / 红辣椒圈1茶匙 / 蒜蓉1茶匙
腌料	老抽2汤匙 / 生抽1汤匙
调味	糖2茶匙

Ingredients	1 duck / 3 sour plums / 4 ginger slices / 2 spring onions 1 tbsp chopped spring onion / 1 tsp red chili rings 1 tsp minced garlic
Marinades	2 tbsps dark soy sauce / 1 tbsp light soy sauce
Seasoning	2 tsps sugar

做法  Method

1. Wash and drain the duck. Marinade for 30 minutes, put spring onions and ginger slices into duck.

2. Discard cores of sour plums, mince with a fork in bowl.

3. Place the steam rack into the wok, add water to nearly the height of the rack. Boil the water, steam the duck over high heat 30-40 minutes till cooked. Cut into pieces after it cools down a little bit.

4. Heat oil in wok, sauté red chili rings and minced garlic, add sour plums and seasonings. Pour over the duck meat after cooked. Dash shredded spring onion and serve.

1. 米鸭洗净，沥干水分，用腌料腌30分钟，将葱段和姜片放入鸭腔内。

2. 梅子去核，放碗中用叉搓成蓉。

3. 在锅中放蒸架，加水至接近蒸架高度，烧滚水，将米鸭用大火隔水蒸30~40分钟至熟，稍凉后起肉切片。

4. 烧热油锅，爆香红辣椒圈和蒜蓉，加入梅子和调味料，煮滚后淋在鸭肉上，洒上葱花即成。

家禽 Poultry

美食达人心动试味 / Gourmet's Comments

冬菇够入味，蚝油味不能太重，否则盖过冬菇味。
Tasty mushrooms. Taste of oyster sauce should not be too rich, otherwise it'd overshadow mushrooms.

Steamed chicken and ham with mushroom
鲜鸡云腿冬菇块

⏱ 25 分钟 / Minutes　　👥 6 人 / Persons

Tips

1. 冬菇要放在密封的器皿内，再置于干燥的地方贮存。
Store dried black mushrooms in sealed container and keep in a dry place.

2. 冬菇用生粉搓洗净，可使色泽更鲜明。
Rub dried black mushrooms with caltrop starch and rinse and it will look better.

材料　　鲜鸡腿2只／冬菇3只／云腿10片
腌料　　盐1汤匙／生抽2茶匙／生粉1茶匙／米酒1茶匙
　　　　姜汁1茶匙／糖½茶匙
调味　　蚝油1茶匙／生抽1茶匙／糖½茶匙／生粉½茶匙

Ingredients: 2 fresh chicken legs / 3 dried black mushrooms / 10 Yunnan ham slices
Marinades: 1 tbsp salt / 2 tsps light soy sauce / 1 tsp caltrop starch
1 tsp rice wine / 1 tsp ginger juice / ½ tsp sugar
Seasonings: 1 tsp oyster oil / 1 tsp light soy sauce / ½ tsp sugar
½ tsp caltrop starch

做法

1. Wash chicken legs, Marinade for 5 minutes. Chop into pieces.
2. Soak dried black mushrooms till soft, remove stalks and wash. Wash the ham and drain.
3. Put chicken, ham and mushrooms alternately on dish, mix seasonings in bowl. Pour it over chicken, ham and mushrooms.
4. Place the steam rack into the wok, add water to nearly the height of the rack. Boil the water, steam the chicken over high heat about 12 minutes. Serve.

1. 鸡腿洗净，用腌料腌5分钟，斩块。
2. 冬菇提前浸软，去蒂，洗净。云腿洗净，沥干水分。
3. 将鸡块、云腿、冬菇按序相间地排在蒸碟上，将调味料在碗中拌匀，淋在鸡块、云腿、冬菇上。
4. 在锅中放蒸架，加水至接近蒸架高度，烧滚水，将鸡块用大火隔水蒸约12分钟即成。

Poultry

美食达人心动试味 / *Gourmet's Comments*

蛋质嫩滑。蒸的时间不能太久,否则蛋会变得老而不滑。
Don't cook for too long and the egg will be smooth, otherwise it will be overdone.

Steamed egg with dried shrimp
虾米蒸水蛋

⏱ 20 分钟 / Minutes   👥 4 人 / Persons

Tips

1 烧滚水后需要转中火。
Turn to medium heat after the water is boiled.

2 用牙签刺入水蛋,可测试是否已熟。
Poke a toothpick into steamed egg to see if it's cooked.

材料	虾米1汤匙 / 鸡蛋3只
调味料	生抽2茶匙

Ingredients	1 tbsp dried shrimps / 3 eggs
Marinade	2 tsps light soy sauce

做法  Method

1. Soak dried shrimps till soft. Wash and drain.
2. Put egg in big bowl, add the same amount of water, mix with seasonings. Pour into deep dish, cover with aluminum foil.
3. Place the steam rack into the wok, add water to nearly the height of the rack. Boil the water, steam the egg over medium heat about 8 minutes till cooked. Serve.

1. 虾米浸软,洗净,沥干水分。
2. 鸡蛋放大碗中,加相同分量水拌匀,下调味料拌匀,倒进深蒸碟中,盖上锡纸。
3. 在锅中放蒸架,加水至接近蒸架高度,烧滚水,将鸡蛋用中火隔水蒸8分钟至熟即成。

Poultry

美食达人心动试味 / *Gourmet's Comments*

蛋质嫩滑,海鲜色泽鲜艳。可用其他海鲜,如带子、蚬肉,但要注意颜色搭配。
Smooth egg and colorful seafood. Shrimps could be substituted by other seafood like scallop and clam. But pay attention to the matching of colors.

Steamed cup custard with seafood
海鲜茶碗蒸

18 分钟 / Minutes **2** 人 / Persons

Tips

鸡蛋拌匀后,先放5分钟再蒸,待鸡蛋中的空气排出,可使鸡蛋较滑。

After mixing the egg, wait for 5 minutes before steaming. The egg will be smoother as bubbles in egg are gone.

材料 蟹柳1条 / 虾仁4只 / 鸡蛋2只 / 清鸡汤¾杯
调味料 生抽1茶匙

Ingredients 1 crab stick / 4 shrimps / 2 eggs / ¾ cup chicken broth
Seasoning 1 tsp light soy sauce

做法  Method

1. Wash and drain crab stick, tear into strips.
2. Wash and drain shrimps. Steam shrimps over high heat about 5 minutes till cooked, shell.
3. Mix eggs in big bowl, blend with chicken broth, pour into two cups, cover with aluminum foil.
4. Place the steam rack into the wok, add water to nearly the height of the rack. Boil the water, steam the cup custards over high heat about 6 minutes till 80% cooked. Take out.
5. Place shrimps and crab stick strips on egg surface. Steam for another 2 minutes till cooked, pour light soy sauce and serve.

1. 蟹柳洗净,沥干水分,撕成丝。
2. 虾仁洗净,沥干水分。将虾仁用大火隔水蒸约5分钟至熟,去壳。
3. 鸡蛋在大碗中打匀,加入清鸡汤拌匀,倒入两个碗中,盖上锡纸。
4. 在锅中放蒸架,加水至接近蒸架高度,烧滚水,将海鲜茶碗用大火隔水蒸约6分钟至八成熟,取出。
5. 将虾仁、蟹柳丝放在鸡蛋上面,再蒸2分钟至熟,淋上生抽即成。

Pork and Beef

美食达人心动试味 / Gourmet's Comments

梅菜味道适中，糖不能下太多，否则会太甜。
To make preserved cabbage right, don't add too much sugar or it will be too sweet.

Steamed pork slice with preserved cabbage
梅菜蒸肉片

⏱ 15 分钟 / Minutes   👥 4~6 人 / Persons

Tips

1. 梅菜有咸与甜之分，若用咸梅菜便要加些糖拌匀。
There are salty and sweet preserved cabbage, add some sugar and mix well if it's sweet preserved cabbage.

2. 梅菜中有沙粒，必须撕开菜夹洗净。
There are sands in preserved cabbage, tear it open and wash.

材料	瘦梅头猪肉300克 / 甜梅菜1棵
猪肉腌料	玉米淀粉粉½茶匙
梅菜腌料	糖1茶匙 / 油少许

Ingredients	300g lean tenderloin pork / 1 stalk sweet preserved cabbage
Marinades	for pork: ½ tsp corn starch
	for preserved cabbage: 1 tsp sugar / some oil

做法  Method

1. Wash the lean tenderloin pork and drain. Slice, add pork marinade and mix well.

2. Put sweet preserved cabbage into water and soak for a while. Wash and drain, cut into slices.

3. Heat the wok, stir-fry preserved cabbage dices slightly, take out and add preserved cabbage marinade, mix well.

4. Blend tenderloin pork and preserved cabbage, place it on dish flat.

5. Place the steam rack into the wok, add water to nearly the height of the rack. Boil the water, steam the pork over high heat for about 7 minutes. Serve.

1. 梅头猪肉洗净，沥干水分，切片，加猪肉腌料拌匀。

2. 甜梅菜用水浸片刻，洗净，沥干水分，切粒。

3. 烧热锅，以白锅略炒（即不加油）梅菜粒，盛起，加梅菜腌料拌匀。

4. 梅头猪肉与梅菜拌匀，平放蒸碟上。

5. 在锅中放蒸架，加水至接近蒸架高度，烧滚水，将梅菜猪肉用大火隔水蒸约7分钟即成。

美食达人心动试味 / Gourmet's Comments

肉饼嫩滑，马蹄有质感，但不要太大粒。
Smooth minced pork and crunchy water chestnut. The dice should not be too big.

Steamed minced pork with dried squid
土鱿蒸肉饼

⏱ 18 分钟 / Minutes   👥 4~6 人 / Persons

Tips

1. 搅拌绞猪肉要沿同一个方向搅，否则不易起胶。
   Blend the minced pork in one direction, or else it won't be elastic.

2. 搅好的肉饼可加½只蛋白，可使肉饼较滑且不会收缩。
   Add ½ egg white into the minced pork to make it smoother, so it won't shrink easily.

材料　绞猪肉300克／土鱿3只／冬菇3只／马蹄3粒
腌料　生抽2茶匙／糖½茶匙／玉米淀粉2茶匙

Ingredients　300g minced pork／3 dried squids／3 dried black mushrooms／3 water chestnuts
Marinades　2 tsps light soy sauce／½ tsp sugar／2 tsps corn starch

做法  Method

1. Soak dried squids till soft, tear off the soft bones. Drain and cut into dice. Peel water chestnuts.
2. Soak dried black mushrooms till soft, wash and remove stalks. Drain and cut into dice. Peel water chestnuts and wash. Drain and cut into dice.
3. Place minced pork in a big bowl, add marinades and mix in one direction till elastic. And then add other ingredients and mix, put it on dish flat.
4. Place the steam rack into the wok, add water to nearly the height of the rack. Boil the water, steam the pork over high heat for about 8 minutes. Serve.

1. 土鱿提前浸软，撕去软骨，沥干水分，切粒。
2. 冬菇提前浸软，洗净，去蒂，沥干水分，切粒。马蹄去皮洗净，沥干水分，切粒。
3. 绞猪肉放大碗中，加腌料拌匀，沿同一个方向打至起胶，再加入其他材料拌匀，平铺在蒸碟上。
4. 在锅中放蒸架，加水至接近蒸架高度，烧滚水，将土鱿肉饼用大火隔水蒸约8分钟即成。

Pork and Beef

美食达人心动试味 / *Gourmet's Comments*

要使牛肉松身软滑,一定要横纹逆切。
To have smooth and soft beef, cross cut.

Steamed beef with preserved vegetable
榨菜蒸牛肉

⏱ 20 分钟 / Minutes 👥 4 人 / Persons

Tips

腌牛肉时加点水,可令牛肉松软、嫩滑。
Add water when marinating beef to make it smooth and soft.

材料　　　牛肉300克／榨菜1小块
牛肉腌料　生抽2茶匙／玉米淀粉1茶匙／糖½茶匙
榨菜腌料　糖1茶匙／麻油1茶匙

Ingredients 300g beef / 1 small piece preserved vegetable
Marinades　for beef: 2 tsps light soy sauce / 1 tsp corn starch / ½ tsp sugar
　　　　　for preserved vegetable: 1 tsp sugar / 1 tsp sesame oil

做法 Method

1. Wash preserved vegetable and drain, cut into thin slices, add preserved vegetable marinade and mix well.

2. Wash beef and drain, slice. Add beef marinades and wait 5 minutes, add 1 tbsp of water and blend, Marinade for another 5 minutes.

3. Place preserved vegetable and beef alternately on dish.

4. Place the steam rack into the wok, add water to nearly the height of the rack. Boil the water, steam the beef over high heat for about 5 minutes. Serve.

1. 榨菜洗净，沥干水分，切薄片，加榨菜腌料拌匀。

2. 牛肉洗净，沥干水分，切片，加牛肉腌料腌5分钟，加1汤匙水拌匀，再腌5分钟。

3. 榨菜和牛肉相间排在蒸碟上。

4. 在锅中放蒸架，加水至接近蒸架高度，烧滚水，将榨菜牛肉用大火隔水蒸约5分钟即成。

猪年 Pork and Beef

美食达人心动试味 / Gourmet's Comments

排骨肉质爽滑、入味，可加红椒丝增加辣味和色彩。
Crunchy, smooth and tasty spareribs. To make it spicier and more colorful, add shredded red chilies.

Steamed spare ribs in black bean sauce
豉汁蒸排骨

⏱ 50 分钟 / Minutes 👥 4~6 人 / Persons

Tips

清洗排骨时，放水龙头下冲洗，可令肉质较爽。
Rinse spareribs under running tap to make it crunchier.

| 材料 | 排骨300克 / 豆豉1汤匙 |
| 腌料 | 蒜蓉2茶匙 / 姜蓉1茶匙 / 生抽1茶匙 / 玉米淀粉1茶匙 / 糖½茶匙 / 油½茶匙 / 胡椒粉少许 |

| Ingredients | 300g spareribs / 1 tbsp black beans |
| Marinades | 2 tsps minced garlic / 1 tsp minced ginger / 1 tsp light soy sauce 1 tsp cornstarch / ½ tsp sugar / ½ tsp oil / some pepper |

做法

1. Wash black beans and drain, chop.
2. Wash spareribs and drain.
3. Add the mashed black beans into spareribs, Marinade for 25 minutes. Put spareribs on dish.
4. Place the steam rack into the wok, add water to nearly the height of the rack. Boil the water, steam the spare ribs over high heat for about 15 minutes. Serve.

1. 豆豉洗净,沥干水分,剁碎。
2. 排骨洗净,沥干水分。
3. 将豆豉碎加入排骨中,再下腌料腌25分钟,将排骨排在蒸碟上。
4. 在锅中放蒸架,加水至接近蒸架高度,烧滚水,将排骨用大火隔水蒸约15分钟即成。

Pork and Beef

美食达人心动试味 / Gourmet's Comments

豆腐嫩滑。弄成大小一样的豆腐小块,加上葱花点缀,可增加食欲。
Smooth beancurd. Cut into small slices of same size, add shredded spring onion to make it appetizing.

Steamed beancurd with minced pork
肉碎蒸豆腐

⏱ 40 分钟 / Minutes   👥 4~6 人 / Persons

Tips

1. 若用盒装豆腐,要选用蒸豆腐。
   Use steam beancurd if it's boxed beancurd.
2. 可焯些蔬菜伴碟。
   Boiled vegetables could be added as side dish.

| 材料 | 绞猪肉150克 / 豆腐1块 / 葱花1茶匙 / 油2汤匙 |
| 腌料 | 老抽1茶匙 / 盐½茶匙 / 糖½茶匙 / 生粉½茶匙 |

| Ingredients | 150g minced pork / 1 piece beancurd / 1 tsp shredded spring onion / 2 tbsps oil |
| Marinades | 1 tsp dark soy sauce / ½ tsp salt / ½ tsp sugar / ½ tsp caltrop starch |

做法 Method

1. Marinade minced pork for 20 minutes.
2. Wash beancurd and drain, cut into small pieces.
3. Put the beancurd on dish, place minced pork on top.
4. Place the steam rack into the wok, add water to nearly the height of the rack. Boil the water, steam the minced pork and beancurd over high heat for about 10 minutes. Add shredded spring onion.
5. Heat 2 tbsps of oil, turn off the heat. Pour over minced pork and beancurd. Serve.

1. 绞猪肉加腌料腌20分钟。
2. 豆腐洗净，沥干水分，切小块。
3. 豆腐排放在蒸碟上，铺上绞猪肉。
4. 在锅中放蒸架，加水至接近蒸架高度，烧滚水，将肉碎豆腐用大火隔水蒸约10分钟，洒上葱花。
5. 另烧热2汤匙油，熄火，淋在肉碎豆腐上即成。

美食达人心动试味 / Gourmet's Comments

肉丸爽口，有咸鱼香味，咸鱼不能太多，否则太咸。
Crunchy meat balls with aromatic salted fish. Don't add too much salted fish or else it'll too salty.

Steamed salted fish with meat ball
咸鱼蒸肉丸

⏱ 30 分钟 / Minutes   👥 4 人 / Persons

Tips

1 若用梅香咸鱼便不用煎香。
No need to stir-fry if Mui Heong salted fish is used.

2 猪肉搅拌后再用手挞向碗中，更易起胶。
Smash minced meat into the bowl with hands to make it elastic.

材料　梅头猪肉250克／咸鱼1小块／马蹄4粒／姜蓉1茶匙
腌料　鸡蛋白1只／水2茶匙／油1茶匙／生粉1茶匙／糖1/3茶匙
　　　盐1/3茶匙／胡椒粉1/3茶匙

Ingredients　250g tenderloin pork / 1 small piece of salted fish / 4 water chestnuts / 1 tsp minced ginger

Marinades　1 egg white / 2 tsps water / 1 tsp oil / 1 tsp caltrop starch / 1/3 tsp sugar / 1/3 tsp salt / 1/3 pepper

做法 Method

1. Wash tenderloin pork and drain. Put into a big bowl after chopped, add marinades and stir till elastic.

2. Peel water chestnuts and wash. Drain and cut into dice.

3. Wash salted fish and drain.

4. Heat oil in wok, shallow-fry salted fish till browned. Take out, remove bones after cooling down and then strip.

5. Put all ingredients in big bowl and blend in one direction till elastic. Squeeze out meat balls with hands, put on the dish.

6. Place the steam rack into the wok, add water to nearly the height of the rack. Boil the water, steam the meat ball over high heat for about 15 minutes. Serve.

1. 梅头猪肉洗净，沥干水分，剁碎后放大碗中，加腌料搅拌至起胶。

2. 马蹄去皮，洗净，沥干水分，切粒。

3. 咸鱼洗净，沥干水分。

4. 烧热油锅，下咸鱼煎至金黄，盛起，待凉后起肉，切碎。

5. 将所有材料放大碗中拌匀，顺一个方向拌至起胶，用虎口挤出肉丸，排放在蒸碟上。

6. 在锅中放蒸架，加水至接近蒸架高度，烧滚水，将咸鱼肉丸用大火隔水蒸约15分钟即可。

美食达人心动试味 / Gourmet's Comments

冬菇要够软够入味，应选大小相似的。
To make soft and tasty dried black mushrooms, they must be in similar size.

Stuffed dried mushrooms
酿冬菇

25 分钟 / Minutes 4 人 / Persons

Tips

1. 免治猪肉（绞碎猪肉），以细切大剁的方式剁成，较用搅拌机搅出的有口感。
Mouthtaste of minced pork would be better if it's chopped from slices compared with those made by machine.

2. 挞猪肉前，先放冰箱冷藏一会，会较易起胶。
Before smashing the pork, put it into a fridge for a while, it'd be easier to make it elastic.

材料	花菇8只 / 梅头猪肉80克
猪肉腌料	生抽1茶匙 / 糖½茶匙 / 玉米淀粉½茶匙
冬菇腌料	生粉1茶匙 / 油1茶匙 / 糖½茶匙
芡汁料	清鸡汤3汤匙 / 蚝油1汤匙 / 玉米淀粉2茶匙 / 麻油1茶匙

Ingredients	8 dried black mushrooms / 80g tenderloin pork
Marinades	for pork: 1 tsp light soy sauce / ½ tsp sugar / ½ tsp cornstarch for black mushroom: 1 tsp caltrop starch / 1 tsp oil / ½ tsp sugar
Thickenings	3 tbsps chicken broth / 1 tbsp oyster oil 2 tsps cornstarch / 1 tsp sesame oil

做法

1. Soak dried black mushrooms till soft, remove stalks. Wash and drain. Add dried black mushroom marinades and mix well.

2. Wash tenderloin pork and drain. Put into a big bowl after chopped, add pork marinades and stir in one direction till elastic.

3. Stuff the minced tenderloin pork into dried black mushrooms, then place on dish.

4. Place the steam rack into the wok, add water to nearly the height of the rack. Boil the water, steam the stuffed shiitake mushrooms over high heat about 15 minutes. Turn off the heat.

5. Mix thickenings in bowl. Heat oil in wok, pour in the thickening and cook. Pour on stuffed dried black mushrooms and serve.

1. 冬菇（提前）浸软，去蒂，洗净，沥干水分，加冬菇腌料略腌。

2. 梅头猪肉洗净，沥干水分，剁碎后放大碗中，加猪肉腌料顺一个方向搅拌至起胶。

3. 将梅头猪肉碎酿在冬菇中，排放在蒸碟上。

4. 在锅中放蒸架，加水至接近蒸架高度，烧滚水，将酿冬菇用大火隔水蒸约15分钟，熄火。

5. 芡汁料放碗中拌匀。另烧热油锅，下芡汁料煮滚，淋在酿冬菇上即成。

Vegetables

美食达人心动试味 / *Gourmet's Comments*

肉片够入味，够爽口。要选肥瘦相间的猪肉。
Crunchy and tasty pork slices. Pick medium fat pork.

Steamed salted pork in winter melon sandwich
咸猪肉蒸冬瓜夹

⏱ 30 分钟 / Minutes 👥 4 人 / Persons

Tips

1 冬瓜中央所切的一刀不要切到底，否则不能夹实咸猪肉。
Don't cut to the bottom of winter melon, otherwise it can't hold the salted pork.

2 将半肥瘦猪肉加粗盐腌过夜，即成咸猪肉。
Marinade the medium fat pork with coarse salt overnight, it'll become salted pork.

材料　冬瓜400克／咸猪肉200克／清鸡汤1杯
芡汁料　蚝油1汤匙／玉米淀粉2茶匙／糖½茶匙／水3汤匙

Ingredients　400g winter melon / 200g salted pork / 1 cup chicken broth
Thickenings　1 tbsp oyster sauce / 2 tsps cornstarch / ½ tsp sugar / 3 tbsps water

做法  Method

1. Wash winter melon and drain. Peel and cut into the pieces, and then cut in the middle but do not cut to the bottom.
2. Slice salted pork, stuff into the middle of winter melon sandwich, place on dish in order and pour in chicken broth.
3. Place the steam rack into the wok, add water to nearly the height of the rack. Boil the water, steam the winter melon sandwich over high heat for about 15 minutes. Turn off the heat, pour out the sauce.
4. Mix thickening in bowl, add the sauce and mix.
5. Heat oil in wok, add thickening ingredients and cook till it thickens. Rinse on winter melon sandwich and serve.

1. 冬瓜洗净，沥干水分，去皮，切成长方块，在中央直切一刀。
2. 咸猪肉切片，酿入冬瓜夹中，排在深蒸碟上，倒入清鸡汤。
3. 在锅中放蒸架，加水至接近蒸架高度，烧滚水，将冬瓜夹用大火隔水蒸约15分钟，熄火，倒出汁液。
4. 芡汁料放碗中拌匀，加入汁液拌匀。
5. 另烧热油锅，下芡汁料煮至浓稠，淋在冬瓜夹上即成。

美食达人心动试味 / Gourmet's Comments

酿进莲藕的肉碎分量要适中。
Appropriate amount of minced meat in lotus root slices.

Steamed stuffed lotus root slices
酿藕片

50 Minutes   **2** Persons

Tips

酿肉时可利用筷子将肉碎塞进莲藕孔中。
Stuff minced meat into holes of lotus root with chopsticks.

材料	莲藕1节 / 免治猪肉（绞碎猪肉）80克 / 葱1条
腌料	盐1茶匙 / 生抽½茶匙 / 糖½茶匙 / 生粉½茶匙 / 油1茶匙
芡汁料	蚝油2汤匙 / 生粉2茶匙 / 清水3汤匙 / 麻油少许

Ingredients	1 lotus root section / 80g minced pork / 1 spring onion
Marinades	1 tsp salt / ½ tsp light soy sauce / ½ tsp sugar / ½ tsp caltrop starch / 1 tsp oil
Thickenings	2 tbsps oyster sauce / 2 tsps caltrop starch / 3 tbsps water / some sesame oil

做法

1. Cut both ends of lotus root, cook in boiling water for 8 minutes, take out and drain. Wait till cool.

2. Marinade minced pork for 10 minutes, and then stuff into lotus root.

3. Steam lotus root for 10 minutes, cut after cooling down.

4. Heat 1 tbsp of oil, sauté spring onion till aromatic. Add thickening sauce and cook till it thickens. Pour on lotus root slices.

1. 莲藕洗净切齐头尾，放入滚水中煮8分钟，取出沥干水，待凉。

2. 免治猪肉下腌料腌10分钟，然后将肉碎酿入莲藕孔中。

3. 莲藕隔水蒸10分钟，晾凉后切片。

4. 烧热1汤匙油，爆香葱，下芡汁，煮至浓稠，淋在藕片上。

美食达人心动试味 / Gourmet's Comments

茄子有蒜蓉味道,生抽要适量。
Eggplant with aroma of minced garlic. Right amount of light soy sauce.

Steamed eggplant with minced garlic
蒜蓉蒸茄子

12 分钟 / Minutes　　4 人 / Persons

Tips

1. 蒜蓉可不爆香,直接放茄子上蒸。
The garlic could be placed on eggplant to steam directly.

2. 茄子切开后,蒸煮前要放盐水中浸泡,可保持色泽鲜艳。
After cutting eggplant, soak in salt water before steaming too keep it colorful.

材料	茄子1条 / 蒜蓉1½汤匙 / 葱花1汤匙
芡汁料	生抽2茶匙 / 麻油1茶匙

Ingredients	1 eggplant / 1½ tbsps minced garlic / 1 tbsp chopped spring onion
Thickenings	2 tsps light soy sauce / 1 tsp sesame oil

做法 Method

1. Wash and drain eggplant, cut into halves.

2. Place the steam rack into the wok, add water to nearly the height of the rack. Boil water, steam the eggplant over high heat about 6 minutes. Take out.

3. Spread chopped spring onion and add sesame oil.

4. Heat oil in wok, sauté minced garlic till aromatic, turn off the heat. Add light soy sauce and mix, pour on eggplant and serve.

1. 茄子洗净，沥干水分，开边。

2. 在锅中放蒸架，加水至接近蒸架高度，烧滚水，将茄子用大火隔水蒸约6分钟，取出。

3. 洒下葱花，下麻油。

4. 烧热油锅，下蒜蓉爆香，熄火，加生抽拌匀，淋在茄子上即成。

Vegetables

美食达人心动试味 / Gourmet's Comments

本菇菇味清香，竹荪卷长度宜平均，卖相会较好。
Aromatic shimeji mushrooms. It'll look better if bamboo fungus rolls are in the same length.

Steamed bamboo fungus roll with shimeji mushroom
本菇竹荪卷

⏱ 20 分钟 / Minutes 👥 4 人 / Persons

Tips

竹荪浸软后，要剪去尾部。
Cut the end of bamboo fungus after soaking.

材料	本菇1盒（200克） / 竹荪8条 / 蟹柳3条 / 胡萝卜丝2汤匙 / 粉丝少许
腌料	盐½茶匙 / 糖¼茶匙 / 麻油少许
芡汁料	清鸡汤½杯 / 生粉2茶匙 / 盐½茶匙 / 麻油少许 / 胡椒粉少许

Ingredients	1 box of shimeji mushroom (200g) / 8 bamboo fungus / 3 crab sticks 2 tbsps shredded carrot / some vermicelli
Marinades	½ tsp salt / ¼ tsp sugar / some sesame oil
Thickenings	½ cup chicken broth / 2 tsps caltrop starch / ½ tsp salt some sesame oil / some pepper

做法 Method

1. Wash and drain bamboo fungus, cut both ends and cut into pieces.
2. Discard stalks of shimeji mushrooms. Wash and drain.
3. Soak vermicelli till soft and drain. Cut into sections. Add shredded crab stick and carrot, mix well.
4. Heat the wok, boil chicken broth, add bamboo fungus and cook for a while, take out.
5. Arrange bamboo fungus on dish, and place vermicelli, shredded crab stick and carrot on bamboo fungus. Roll up and fix tight with toothpicks.
6. Place the steam rack into the wok, add water to nearly the height of the rack. Boil the water, steam the bamboo fungus over high heat about 4 minutes. Take out and pour out the sauce.
7. Heat oil in wok, slightly stir-fry shimeji mushroom, add thinkening ingredients, mix and cook, rinse on bamboo fungus and serve.

1. 竹荪浸软洗净，沥干水分，剪去头尾，剪成块状。
2. 本菇（本占地菇）去蒂，洗净，沥干水分。
3. 粉丝浸软，沥干水分，切段，加入蟹柳丝、胡萝卜丝和腌料拌匀。
4. 烧热锅，加入清鸡汤煮滚，加入竹荪煨片刻，盛起。
5. 竹荪块铺在碟上，将粉丝、蟹柳丝和胡萝卜丝放在竹荪上，卷成筒状，可用牙签固定。
6. 在锅中放蒸架，加水至接近蒸架高度，烧滚水，将竹荪卷用大火隔水蒸约4分钟，取出，倒出汁液。
7. 烧热油锅，下本菇略炒，加入芡汁料拌匀煮滚，淋在竹荪上即成。

Vegetables

美食达人心动试味 / *Gourmet's Comments*

竹荪卷有冬菇香味,有蚝油味,但蚝油味不能太浓。
Bamboo fungus roll with aromatic dried black mushrooms and oyster sauce. Oyster sauce taste should not be too rich.

Steamed stuffed bamboo fungus
三宝酿竹荪

⏱ 15 分钟 / Minutes 👥 4~6 人 / Persons

Tips

1. 所有材料的长度要均一,较美观。
   All ingredients should be of the same length.
2. 芦笋只用顶部。
   Just use the top of asparagus.

材料　竹荪10条／火腿1片／芦笋25克／冬菇3只
芡汁料　清鸡汤¼杯／蚝油2茶匙／糖1茶匙

Ingredients　10 bamboo fungus／1 piece ham／25g asparagus／3 dried black mushrooms

Thickenings　¼ cup chicken broth／2 tsps oyster sauce／1 tsp sugar

做法

1. Wash and drain bamboo fungus, cut both ends.
2. Soak dried black mushrooms and drain. Discard stalks and shred.
3. Wash ham and asparagus respectively and drain. Strip ham and cut asparagus into sections.
4. Stuff dried black mushrooms, ham and asparagus into bamboo fungus, arrange on dish. Mix thickening in bowl and rinse on bamboo fungus.
5. Place the steam rack into the wok, add water to nearly the height of rack. Boil the water, steam the stuffed bamboo fungus over high heat about 8 minutes and serve.

1. 竹荪浸软洗净，沥干水分，剪去头尾。
2. 冬菇浸软，沥干水分，去蒂，切丝。
3. 火腿、芦笋分别洗净，沥干水分。火腿切条，芦笋切段。
4. 将冬菇、火腿、芦笋各一酿入竹荪内，排在蒸碟上。芡汁料放碗中拌匀，淋在酿竹荪上。
5. 在锅中放蒸架，加水至接近蒸架高度，烧滚水，将酿竹荪用大火隔水蒸约8分钟即成。

蔬菜 / Vegetables

美食达人心动试味 / Gourmet's Comments

豆腐嫩滑，颜色鲜明。皮蛋、咸蛋要切成小粒，令味道与颜色都均匀。
Smooth beancurd and it's colorful. Cut preserved eggs and salted eggs into dice to have savor and color well mixed.

Steamed preserved eggs with beancurd
金银蛋蒸豆花

⏱ 15 分钟 / Minutes   👥 4~6 人 / Persons

Tips

1. 皮蛋烚熟（在滚水中煮熟）后较易切粒。
   It's easier to cut preserved egg into dice after boiling.

2. 鸡蛋烚熟后，立即浸在凉水中冷却，较易除壳。
   After boiling, put the egg into cold water immediately and it'd be easier to shell.

材料　软豆腐1块 / 鸡蛋1只 / 咸蛋1只 / 皮蛋1只 / 葱花1茶匙
调味　生抽2茶匙 / 盐1茶匙 / 生粉1茶匙 / 油1茶匙

Ingredients　1 piece soft beancurd / 1 egg / 1 salted egg / 1 preserved egg / 1 tsp chopped spring onion
Seasonings　2 tsps light soy sauce / 1 tsp salt / 1 tsp caltrop starch / 1 tsp oil

做法 Method

1. Wash salted egg, preserved egg. Mix the egg well.

2. Heat a pot of water, boil salted egg and preserved egg and then take out. Soak and cool in cold water. Shell and cut into dice.

3. Wash the beancurd and drain. Mince and add seasonings, egg, salted egg and preserved egg to blend well, put on dish flat.

4. Place the steam rack into the wok, add water to nearly the height of rack. Boil the water, steam the beancurd over high heat about 8 minutes. Spray chopped onion.

5. Heat oil and turn off the heat. Add light soy sauce and slightly cook, pour on beancurd and serve.

1. 咸蛋、皮蛋洗净。鸡蛋打匀。

2. 烧热一锅水，加入咸蛋、皮蛋焓熟，取出，浸在凉水中冷却，除壳，切粒。

3. 豆腐洗净，沥干水分，搅碎，加调味料、鸡蛋、咸蛋和皮蛋粒拌匀，平铺在蒸碟上。

4. 在锅中放蒸架，加水至接近蒸架高度，烧滚水，将豆腐用大火隔水蒸约8分钟，洒上葱花。

5. 烧热油，熄火，下生抽略煮，淋在豆腐上即成。

烹饪小词典
Cooking key words

常用调味品（附广东话发音）
Common seasonings

granulated sugar
砂糖 sa tong

brown sugar
黄糖 wong tong

slab sugar
片糖 pin tong

rock sugar
冰糖 bing tong

salt
盐 yim

corn oil
粟米油 sug mi yeo

olive oil
橄榄油 gem lam yeo

cooking oil
生油 seng yeo

butter
牛油 ngeo yeo

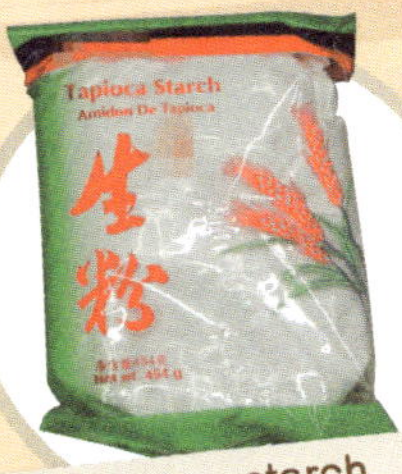

caltrop starch
生粉 seng fen

flour
面粉 min fen

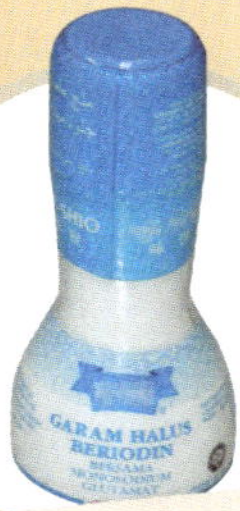

MSG
味精 mei jing

chili bean sauce
豆瓣酱 deo ban zeng

satay sauce
沙嗲酱 sa de zeng

miso
面酱 min zeng

fermented black beans
豆豉 deo xi

red beancurd
南乳 nam yu

fermented beancurd
腐乳 fu yu

black pepper sauce
黑椒烧汁 hak jiu xiu zeb

tabasco
辣椒汁 lad jiu zeb

curry powder
咖喱粉 ga lei fen

chicken powder
鸡粉 gei fen

chicken broth
鸡汤 gei tong

wasabi
芥辣 gai lad

pepper
胡椒粉 wu jiu fen

spices
香料 heng liu

honey
蜜糖 met tong

做菜和味道的常用语
Common phrases of cooking and tastes

普通话Mandarin	英文English	广东话Cantonese（拼音）
食物味道 Taste		
熟	cooked	熟 sug
没熟	raw	未熟 mei sug
生 / 没熟	uncooked	生（未熟）seng
太咸	too salty	太咸 tai ham
太长时间	too long	太耐 tai noi
不够咸	not salty enough	唔够咸 em geo ham
不够甜	not sweet enough	唔够甜 em geo tim
香	aromatic	香 heng
臭	stink	臭 ceo
甜	sweet	甜 tim
酸	sour	酸 xun
苦	bitter	苦 fu
辣	spicy	辣 lad
咸	salty	咸 ham
煮菜方式Cooking Method		
切片	slice	切片 qid pin
切长一点	cut longer	切长少少 qid ceng xiu-xiu
切短一点	cut shorter	切短少少 qid dün xiu-xiu
切块	cut into wedges	切块 qid fai
切粒	cut into dice	切粒粒 qid neb-neb
蒸	steam	蒸 jing
炸	deep-fry	炸 za
煎	shallow-fry	煎 jin
炒菜	stir-fry vegetables	炒菜 cao coi
焯菜	blanch vegetables	渌菜 lug coi
煲汤	cook soup	煲汤 bou tong
焖猪肉	stew pork	炆猪肉 men ju yug

常用技巧
Common skills

切角 Cut into triangles	把物料移动，切成三角形。 Roll the ingredients and cut into triangles.
骨牌 Domino	物料先切成长形，再修切成长方形。 Cut the ingredients into long pieces, and then rectangles.
去衣 Peel off the thin layer	把栗子放滚水中煮1~2分钟，去掉栗子外皮。 Cook chestnuts into boiling water for 1-2 minutes, peel off the thin layer of chestnuts.
去皮 Shave	用刨子削去物料外皮。 Shave off the skin of the ingredients.
料头 Side ingredients	泛指姜、葱、蒜、红葱头或辣椒，协助提升物料的香味。 Usually refer to ginger, spring onion, garlic, shallot and chili which make ingredients more aromatic.
泡油 Blanch with oil	将物料放入八成滚的油中2~3分钟，取出沥油。 Cook ingredients in 80% boiled oil for 2-3 minutes, take out and drain.
飞水（焯一下） Blanch	物料放入滚水中焯2~3分钟，取出过冷（水）。 Cook ingredients in boiling water for 2-3 minutes, take out and rinse with cold water.
白镬（锅） Wok without adding oil	没有添加任何物料、酱料或油等，只是把镬（锅）烧热后直接下物料烘干水分。 Without any ingredients, sauce or oil, dry the ingredients in a heated wok directly.
爆香 Sauté	用少量油加热，放入料头略煎至出味的程序。 Slightly shallow-fry side ingredients till aromatic with some heated oil.